365

Funny

Facts

For

Your

Unfunny

Father

Vol.2

365 Funny Facts For Your Unfunny Father

Vol. 2

Jokes written by: Andrew Rose

(A few by my buddy Ben Flint)

365 Funny Facts For Your Unfunny Father Vol. 2

Copyright @2019 Andrew Rose

Published by Andrew rose

Published Andrew Rose 2018

CONTENTS

Forward!!!

Ok so basically this is where you're supposed to put the information for the book and all that fancy stuff as to why I wanted to make the book.

Well it's in my last book and to be honest I don't feel like typing it up again, so I am not going to. So, if you want to read it buy the other book or just text me (my number is at the end of the book) and ask me about the last books forward.

I will say this.....this shit gets tiring. I completely stopped posting my jokes in January and February and then picked it back up in March to fulfil whatever commitment I gave to myself to the followers on my Instagram, but damn if it wasn't hard work.

Also, ALWAYS ASK THE QUESTION!!!

No matter the question is, ask it, you will always be better having the knowledge, good or bad, than not having it. Ask that other person out on a date, ask your waiter for a discount or a free dessert, at a minimum they'll say no, and at a maximum you'll be on a date with a lovely person who'll get a discounted dessert.

If you don't believe me ask my buddy Josh.

365
Funny
Facts
For
Your
Unfunny
Father
Vol.2

Galileo was still alive when Harvard University was founded.

So, if it hadn't been founded, he may still be alive.

Shirley Temple was the US ambassador to Ghana from 1974 to 1976.

Until after 1976, when they stopped selling Sprite

Wealthy Egyptians slept with neck supports rather than pillows to preserve their hairstyles.

<u>Which clearly didn't work because now they're all dead.</u>

2/3's of parents sing their children to sleep singing pop music.

<u>Which hasn't gotten them to sleep because the kid has terrible taste in music.</u>

The Greater Wax moth can hear sounds more high pitched than any animal can make.

<u>And the Lesser Wax moth is a bitch.</u>

The inventor of roller skates demonstrated them by skating into a party while playing the violin, then crashing into a huge mirror.

<u>His wife was quoted as saying "Told Ya So."</u>

A cheetah can suffer brain damage if it sprints for more than 30 seconds.

<u>And a cheetah that sprints for only 20 seconds won't make the varsity team.</u>

George Eyser, won three gold's, two silvers and a bronze in the 1904 Olympics while having a wooden leg.

<u>And later that year he received a blue ribbon for best costume as a pirate.</u>

Olympic swimmers routinely pee in the pool.

<u>As does the rest of the planet.</u>

The original purpose of the UN was to win the Second World War.

<u>Ha-ha too bad America won, suck that!!</u>

When the pyramids were built, woolly mammoths were still on earth.

<u>And after they were built the Aliens left.</u>

Charles Darwin and Abraham Lincoln were born on the same day.

<u>And if Lincoln had read Darwin's book then he could have evolved into having a bulletproof skull.</u>

A stressed octopus will often bite off its own limbs.

<u>They should learn to breathe on land and then they could be stress free with their 8 blunts.</u>

By 2019 there will be more Lego figures than people on earth.

<u>Which is why we need more Lego sex-ed classes.</u>

There were only 11 democracies in the world in 1941.

<u>And in 2019 there is only 1…. inside Trumps Brain.</u>

The peak time for moth activity is one o'clock in the morning.

<u>So, if you want to study moths, go outside at 1am and kiss your friends goodbye.</u>

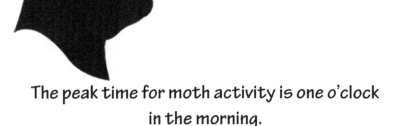

If an area has more rivers, more languages will evolve there.

<u>And the more languages that evolve is directly proportional to people that say, "Huh?", "What? ", "Sorry I don't Speak That."</u>

The sign for the female gender, represents the hand mirror of the Roman Goddess Venus.

<u>Which means that even in god form women are too obsessed with looks.</u>

When threatened, a limpet can run away as fast as 2 inches an hour.

<u>Which is crazy when you realize you don't know what a limpet is.</u>

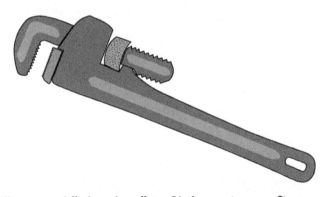

The word "plumber" in Chilean, is gasfitter.

<u>And the Chilean number for 64, is 64.</u>

Sports journalists were banned from the first modern Olympics, since they were considered professional sportspeople.

<u>Which makes sense because of the athletic prowess it takes to use a typewriter.</u>

The most shoplifted food in the UK is Cheese.

<u>The least most shoplifted item is toothpaste.</u>

UN Secretary-General Ban Ki-moon celebrated his election by singing "Ban Ki-moon is coming to town", but to the tune of "Santa Claus Is Coming to town"

<u>But was fired when he changed the line to "I see you when you're seeping."</u>

The original ad for band members for the Village People read, "Macho types wanted: must have mustache."

<u>Unfortunately, Randy Savage was turned down.</u>

The word "British" is the most commonly used term in UK porn.

<u>The Second Most term is imperialism.</u>

Harvey Weinstein had been thanked 12 times at the Oscars, that's once more than God.

<u>And since 2017 he has been thanked for the material at every open mic.</u>

The appropriate response in Luxembourgish
to "How are you?" is "Tip-Top."

<u>Crazy right? Who knew Luxembourgish
was a word.</u>

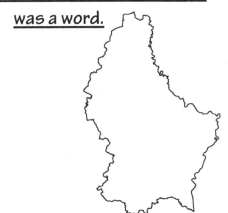

The eyes of a giant squid are about the size
of basketballs.

<u>But they just squish if you dribble
them.</u>

Rene Descartes, the French philosopher, had a fetish for cross-eyed women.

<u>Only since it doubled him in their vision, and he considered that a threesome.</u>

Reindeer have golden eyes in summer and blue eyes in the winter.

<u>And if they have a red nose, it means they did too much cocaine.</u>

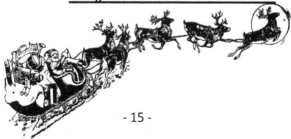

The second episode of The Muppets had the
title "Sex and Violence".

<u>Which is where they introduced Giant
Cock, later renamed Big Bird.</u>

Until the 19th century, champagne was pink
and had no bubbles.

<u>And once they put the bubbles in it,
optometrist appointments rose.</u>

For every leaf there are 340 ants.

<u>Who knew Toronto hockey families
were so huge.</u>

The daddy longlegs flosses after meals by
pulling each of its legs through its jaws.

<u>That's how my uncle flosses, but the
spider hates it.</u>

French toast is over a thousand years older than France.

<u>Before then they called it Cinnamon, Eggy, Sugar bread.</u>

If all the planets fresh water supply disappeared there would be enough left in Russia's Lake Baikal to supply humanity for 50 years.

<u>That is if the Russians don't turn it all to vodka.</u>

If you cry in space your tears won't fall, they will just puddle up under your eye.

<u>And if you cry in the shower, you are me every Tuesday.</u>

Eels can live inside a shark's heart.

<u>They are considered nature's defibrillator.</u>

A salamander can have its brain removed, cut up and put back together again and it will function as normal.

<u>Which begs the question, what kind of sadistic scientists are we letting touch animals.</u>

The body of the sea otter has a pouch across their front that holds rocks to break open shellfish.

<u>My grandpa does the same thing with his hammer toes.</u>

In Brazil, the city "Rio" is pronounced "Hio."

<u>And my ex-step mother Lori is
pronounced Whore-E.</u>

Louis XIV's favorite seasoning was soy sauce.

<u>My cousin in Kentucky's favorite
seasoning is winter.</u>

In 1988 there were over 600,000 illegal gold prospectors in Brazil.

<u>And in 1989 they forgot to count them.</u>

Drinking wine before a meal makes you eat 25% more.

<u>Which explains why my alcoholic aunt is obese.</u>

Hippopotamuses give birth in water.

As do weird hippy chicks.

Gavisti is the Sanskrit word for "war", which literally translates as "desire for more cows"

And in Creole the word "cow" translates as "Aunt Cheryl"

Michael Phelps has won more Olympic gold medals than India, Nigeria, North Korea, Portugal, Taiwan, and Thailand combined.

<u>And when questioned about that fact he was quoted as saying "*cough**cough* Man I'm hungry, who wants Taco Bell?"</u>

When the catering staff at the UN went on strike, over $ 10,000 of silverware and food was stolen.

<u>They couldn't keep track of the silverware and yet we decided to let them try and defeat terrorism...</u>

Jon Bon Jovi used to make Christmas Decorations.

And now he makes awful music.

The annual UK porn industry awards ceremony is called the SHAFTAs.

Which was changed from its original name, the POUNDERs.

90% of all jellyfish are smaller than a human thumbnail.

Which means it will take a long time to collect enough to spread on your toast.

71% of Oscar winners have shed tears since 1995.

And 100% of the losers used their not-good-enough acting chops to pretend they weren't upset.

Nigeria is the world's third largest movie producing country, although it only had 8 cinemas.

I thought they only produced was war lords.

Levi Jeans with copper rivets were priced at $ 13.50 per dozen in 1874.

And if you spend that amount now, you can get one pair of rivets.

Eating over 20 million bananas would give you a fatal dose of radio activity.

Eating over 20 million bananas would give
you a fatal dose of radio activity.

<u>So would a bite from a six-legged
Chernobyl antelope.</u>

Some rats get more depressed in summer
then in the winter.

<u>Sounds like they should hang out with
Templeton and go to the fair.</u>

95% of the spiders in your house have never gone outside

But if I see one I will make sure a man throws them there.

The Royal Navy have used blasts of "Oops I Did it Again" to scare off Somali pirates.

Which will only work until the pirates get a choreographer.

Lake Baikal in in Russia is over a thousand times older than any other lake on earth.

<u>And it uses this fact to bully the other lakes.</u>

The Empress Josephine had a pet orangutan which joined her for dinner dressed in a white cotton blouse.

<u>Big deal my aunt eats with a jackass in a flannel called Uncle John.</u>

In 1986, Michael Foot was appointed as the chair of a disarmament committee which prompted the Times headline to read "Foot Heads Arms Body"

<u>Sometimes life is easy, and you don't need to write a punch line.</u>

The world-record holder of the longest, most accurate archery shot has no arms.

<u>And to pour salt on the wound when it happened, every applauded.</u>

The volume of soy sauce brewed in the Netherlands each year is greater than all the gold mined in human history.

<u>I wonder if their neighbors complain that the volume is too loud.</u>

"Dr. Seuss" should to be pronounced "Dr. Zoice".

<u>The word describing people who believe this is pronounced Loo-Nuh-Tik</u>

Lettuce was sacred to Min, the ancient Egyptian god of fertility, because it grew long, straight, and oozed a milky substance when rubbed.

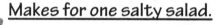
Makes for one salty salad.

Ancient Greeks would declare their love for a woman by throwing an apple at her.

It's the same now if you switch "throwing" for "swiping" and get rid of the "le" in "apple"

James and the Giant Peach was going to be called James and the Giant Cherry.

<u>But a Giant Cherry was just unbelievable.</u>

Twister was first called Pretzel.

<u>And Risk, is something you take when you eat Taco Bell.</u>

In the Boy Scouts' original motto "Be prepared" was followed by "to die for your country."

<u>Now it's followed by "for repressed memories."</u>

The epics of Homer were originally set to music.

<u>And the music was played on Lisa's Saxophone.</u>

Wine Drinkers Pour 12% more wine into a glass they are holding than one sitting on the table.

<u>But only when people are around, if not we just put a straw in the bottle.</u>

Queen Elizabeth I owned 2 "unicorn horns" that apparently purified water and cured sickness.

<u>But they turned out to just be Brita filters.</u>

An Egyptian cure for insanity was to eat snake meatballs under the full moon.

<u>The U.S. cure is electricity.</u>

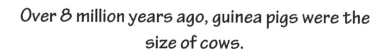

Over 8 million years ago, guinea pigs were the size of cows.

<u>Cows were the size of cows then too.</u>

Franz Liszt was the first musician to have a women's underwear thrown at him.

<u>That's crazy right…. Who the hell is Franz?</u>

The manager of the England soccer team collects mementos of the assassination of president JFK.

<u>HE DID IT!!!</u>

94% of terrorist campaigns have failed to achieve a single one of their strategic goals.

#Bitches (only joking please don't hurt me terrorist people)

Saudi law defines atheists as terrorists.

But the atheists don't believe in that law.

Paro Airport in Bhutan is so dangerous that only 8 pilots have been qualified to land there.

<u>Many more have landed there, but in a fiery blaze.</u>

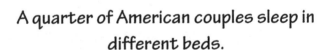

A quarter of American couples sleep in different beds.

<u>And the other ¾'s aren't that super religious.</u>

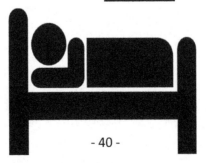

The Japanese sleep two hours less than the Chinese.

<u>Which is why they will get Gundams first.</u>

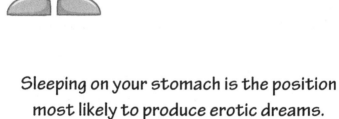

Sleeping on your stomach is the position most likely to produce erotic dreams.

<u>Personal experience says B.S.</u>

The pupils of human eyes are at their biggest as an adolescent and get smaller until the age of 60.

<u>Then they get big again because of your "Glaucoma" medicine.</u>

Einstein's brain was smaller than the average persons.

<u>Goes to show what you can do when you put your smaller than average mind to it.</u>

In the 1930's the US Army drew up plans to invade both Mexico and Canada.

<u>But the plans leaked to Mexico they reverse engineered it, and thus we have a work force.</u>

252 people are born every single minute.

<u>Which means that every hour the planet gets over 30,000 new nipples.</u>

There are beetles named after Darth Vader, Kate Winslet, and even Adolf Hitler.

<u>None of whom can act, but the beetles are cool.</u>

Nachos were created by a man named Nacho.

<u>And are eaten by guys named "duuuuude."</u>

The Father of the founder of Amazon, Jeff Bezos, was a unicyclist in a circus.

<u>The fact that he got laid is astonishing.</u>

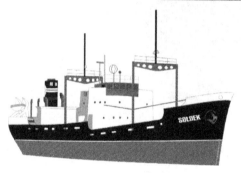

The world's largest container ships can carry over 746 million bananas.

<u>So that's where Mario Kart gets its supply...</u>

New Zealand has an official National Wizard.

<u>So does the KKK.</u>

Greece is the only country; whose name contains none of the letters in the word "Olympiads."

<u>But it does if you're normal and call them the Olympics.</u>

Up until 1910, film studios did not credit actors in case they asked for more money.

<u>And even with the help of technology and lawyers they still can't get the money now, due to being dead.</u>

Jellyfish born on the space shuttle Columbia suffered from vertigo when they returned to Earth.

<u>And those same jellyfish, upon a different re-entry, became crispy.</u>

The ancient Egyptian word for "cat" is pronounced "miaow."

I thought it would have been pronounced "Fuck he scratched me again."

Louis XVI was too fat to fit into the guillotine at his execution.

But he preferred big boned.

A blind person is twice as likely to smell things in their dreams as a sighted person.

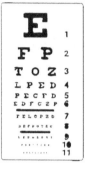

<u>They are also 40x more likely to walk into traffic.</u>

The real Maria von Trapp was not invited to the premiere of The Sound of Music.

<u>Because she was still running from Nazis and couldn't get out of hiding.</u>

The Rubber Ducky, cellophane and the division sign (÷) were all invented in Switzerland.

<u>As were a knife with the ability cut toe nails in battle.</u>

A lully-prigger was an 18th century thief who caught children and then stole their clothing.

<u>Today we call them pedophiles.</u>

The crunch of a potato chip or an apple in your mouth is a mini sonic boom.

<u>Most people just call it a sound...</u>

In 2013 China's only female Mao Zedong impersonator was divorced by her husband who "was tired of feeling that he was sleeping with the chairman."

<u>If only she was a sexy nurse impersonator.</u>

As soon as they find a rock to anchor themselves to, young sea squirts will eat their own brains.

Which makes me wonder what the hell is a sea squirt?

Oliver Cromwell was dug up and beheaded over 2 years after his death.

In case that whole zombie thing panned out.

Fighter Pilots in stressful situations can release such large amounts of hormones that they may ejaculate.

<u>Which is unfortunate since they usually get stressed at the dinner table.</u>

The eyes of the celestial eye goldfish really are bigger than its stomach.

<u>So, when it doesn't clean its plate, it's totally acceptable.</u>

For 500 years from the 13th century, 70% of Englishmen were called Robert, John, Thomas, Richard, or William.

<u>So 14% of them were dicks.</u>

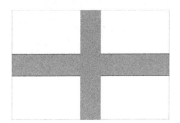

When Danes pose for their photos they say "orange", the Chinese say "aubergine," and The Germans say, "ant shit."

<u>So that's one thing the Germans got right.</u>

In 2009, a search of Loch Ness for the Loch Ness monster located over 100k golf balls.

<u>**Fake News, they were all Nessie Eggs!!**</u>

In 1923 the sheet music for "Yes, We Have No Bananas" sold around 1,000 copies a day.

<u>**The funny thing is they did in fact have bananas!!!**</u>

New Zealand badminton team was named the "Black Cocks," but had to drop it after many complaints.

<u>The complaints were that they weren't called the African Cocks.</u>

There are around 294,000,000,000,000 leaves in the world.

<u>THAT WOULD BE THE BEST PILE OF LEAVES TO JUMP INTO!!!!!</u>

Frogs' legs were eaten in Britain for nearly 7,000 years before they were eaten in France.

<u>Then France took it for a few thousand and were also unable to make it appetizing.</u>

Modern Humans Evolved about 80,000 years after javelins were invented.

<u>Aren't we just splitting hairs...they did have spears.</u>

Anne Boleyn was the only British monarch that was beheaded with a sword.

That is unless queen Elizabeth wants to go out with a bang.

Whales' vaglnas can be large enough to walk through.

As can your moms.

An octopus's limbs contain about two-thirds of its brain.

2/3's of my uncle's brain is unusable after that "Hold My Beer" experiment.

In 2011, Australia minted a giant "A$ 1 Million" gold coin, that weighed over a ton and is wort about A$ 52 million.

It takes one stupid person to spend $52 to make $1.

In 1976, Ron Wayne, co-founder of apple sold his shares for $800; today they would be worth $35 billion.

<u>What a freakin dummy, had he waited a month he could have made like $100 more.</u>

To eat every different variety of apple at a rate of one a day would take around 20 years.

<u>But at least for 20 years you don't have to see a doctor!!</u>

Classical music played in restaurants apparently increases the amount people spend on wine.

<u>EDM played in restaurants increases the tripping.</u>

In the Himalayas, the smoke from burning millipedes is used to treat hemorrhoids.

<u>They call it Preparation H. Imalayas.</u>

23 Nobel prizes for Medicine have been won
because of the research on guinea pigs.

<u>Alfred Nobel's 1st invention, dynamite,
was also tested on guinea pigs.</u>

British fishermen work 17 times harder
than they did in the 1880's, just to catch
the same number of fish.

<u>Cause the current generation are a
bunch of weak bitches.</u>

It's illegal in Saudi Arabia for men to work in a lingerie shop.

The middle east has sexism.... Say it ain't so.

JFK was wearing a corset when he was shot.

So, his death was also a hate crime?

Gurbanguly Berdimuhamedow, the president of Turkmenistan, sacked 30 TV news staffers in 2008 after a cock roach was spotted walking across the set during a bulletin.

<u>Which makes me wonder how the hell you pronounce his name.</u>

The Red Baron's final word was "kaput".

<u>Which is German for "name a pizza after me"</u>

More US Air Force Pilots are training to fly drones than to fly planes.

<u>That's what happens when they recruit from the Call of Duty leaderboards.</u>

Bananas are used to make kimonos.

<u>It would be much easier if they used sewing machines.</u>

The Masters in Lunacy were Victorian officials that investigated whether people claiming to be insane were faking it.

<u>Unofficially they were called Psycho Seekers.</u>

When he enlisted in the army J.R.R. Tolkien's son Michael put down his father's profession as "Wizard".

<u>And soon they are going to make a movie about his military experiences that will be too long and probably split into 3 films.</u>

Over the last 10,000 years Niagara Falls has moved over 7 miles upstream.

<u>And if you walk 7 miles downstream, you will be exhausted.</u>

Iceland gets four-fifths of an inch wider every year.

<u>Big deal my dad gets 2" wider each month.</u>

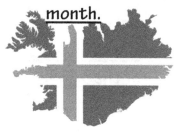

The ice lost in Antarctica every year would be enough to give each person on Earth 1.3million ice cubes.

<u>Including rapper Ice Cube.</u>

Hellenologophobia is the fear of Greek terms.

<u>And Hellenogophobia-phobia is the fear of the people afraid of Greek terms.</u>

The Duke of Wellington played cricket for the country of Ireland.

<u>And his beef dish is delicious.</u>

If you ate in a different New York restaurant every day for 12 years, you still wouldn't have visited all the cities eateries.

<u>And that's when you keep trudging on you pussy.</u>

During its restoration in 1982, the Statue of Liberty's head was accidentally installed about two feet off-center.

<u>So…that's why people think Americans are special.</u>

The guts of over 250k cows were used to make the balloon lining for every Zeppelin.

<u>How cruel…exactly zero cows were harmed in the making of Led Zeppelin 4.</u>

German mothers to be have "roast dinners" not "buns" in their "ovens."

<u>Yea it'd be best if the Germans didn't mention ovens...</u>

Pregreening is creeping forward while waiting for the red light to change.

<u>We just call that typical American driving.</u>

Almost 50% of Alzheimer's patients are between the ages of 75 & 85.

<u>And the other 50% forgot to fill out the age survey.</u>

Louis X and Charles VIII of France both died as a result of playing tennis.

<u>They died of embarrassment due to being caught in those tiny shorts.</u>

Duck-billed platypuses don't have stomachs.

<u>Which is why they don't suffer from acid reflux.</u>

Alternative names proposed for Canada in 1867 were Tuponia, Borealia, and Cabotia.

<u>Also, on the short list was "Oh-I'm-Sorry-Land"</u>

In 1939, the US Army was smaller than the Armies of Portugal or Romania, by 1945 it numbered 8.3 million.

<u>Man, we banged a lot!!</u>

Iceland has 25 puffins for every person.

<u>Damn that's a lot of cereal boxes.</u>

The technical name for an ice-cream headache is sphenopalatine ganglioneuralgia.

Most of us call it an "Awe shit, brain freeze, give me a minute!"

80% of pirates caught by the European Union's naval police are released.

The other 20% are put as extras in Pirates of the Caribbean.

November 25, 2012 was the first day since 1960 that there was no manslaughter in New York City.

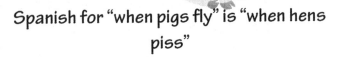

<u>The police were so baffled they almost shot an unarmed white guy, but thought it was in bad taste.</u>

Spanish for "when pigs fly" is "when hens piss"

<u>And that's terrible because, it happens way more often.</u>

Herds of sheep moved at night must have a red light at the back and a white light at the front.

<u>When they can't afford a light, they make Rudolph walk backwards at the end.</u>

There were no traffic rotaries in 1990 in the U.S., now there are more than 3,000.

<u>Goes to show what you can do with time, fortitude, and crippling debt to China.</u>

In the Times, the longest letter ever printed was 11,071 words long.

And the shortest letter is the lowercase "y".

Over 9,000 books are listed as missing from the British Library.

Ironically most of them are the scripts from "Lost."

Davy Crockett was a US congressman.

His campaign slogan was I'm a
Crockett & He's a Crock-A-Shit.

If you made an omelet with all the eggs
produced in a year it would be the size of
Northern Ireland.

So clearly it would be a potato omelet.

Newborn babies of either sex can produce milk.

<u>Well duh. You can milk anything with nipples.</u>

"Bingo" was first used as slang for brandy.

<u>Which means that dog whose Name-O it was, was hammered.</u>

In 1921, a Detroit man killed himself, so he could send a message back from the dead.

...we're still waiting...

A walrus's penis bone is as long as a human thigh bone.

Why is it always the ugly dudes with huge wangs?

There are around 600 men in the world with 2 penises.

<u>And they're the only ones who can have a proper threesome.</u>

90% of people live in the Northern Hemisphere.

<u>Only cause it's closer to Santa's Workshop.</u>

In 2013 the Venezuelan government accused their opposition of causing a national shortage of toilet paper by hoarding it.

It was a shitty time.

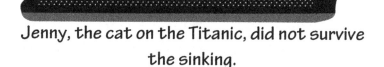

Jenny, the cat on the Titanic, did not survive the sinking.

That's sad since she had to freeze to death 9 times.

Over 200 mice are reported in the houses of parliament each year, and the authorities won't get a cat because no one can be trusted to look after it responsibly.

<u>And yet they are supposed to run a country...</u>

There are more dispensaries in Denver than there are branches of Starbucks.

<u>Only until Starbucks starts selling Coca-Chinos.</u>

Rice Krispies in Germany say "Knisper! Knasper! Knusper!"

KKK...Really?

The energy released by a bolt of lightning is about the same as that stored in about 30 gallons of gasoline.

Which is equal to 1.21 Jigawats!!!

The 45-foot-long V2 rocket carried enough alcohol to make over 66,000 Martinis.

<u>So, the V stands for Vodka.</u>

Pee Cola is a popular soft drink in Ghana.

<u>Oddly it tastes like shit.</u>

The world's largest and most complete T-Rex skeleton is called Sue.

<u>I'd have called her a Tyrano-Sue-Rus-Rex.</u>

Robins' "red" breasts are orange.

<u>Only because Batman made him go tanning.</u>

Fish don't need to learn how to swim in schools.

Because they can take online classes.

A musophobist is a person who distrusts poetry.

And I don't trust musophobists, which makes me.... normal.

Seahorses beat their fins almost as fast as hummingbirds beat their wings.

<u>But if they are put underwater the hummingbird would die.</u>

The 10-spot lady bug has between 0 and 15 spots.

<u>So, it should be the who-knows-how-many-spots ladybug.</u>

The northern hemisphere is three degrees hotter than the southern hemisphere.

<u>Only cause that's where the boobs are.</u>

Predicting the death of Henry VIII was punishable by death.

<u>He predicted his own, which is why he died.</u>

A single sloth can be home to over 900 different beetles.

<u>See Mom, I'm not the only one living off other people!!</u>

There are 20 million sea containers in the world and the ships' crews have no idea what is in them.

<u>It's probably missing Asians.</u>

In China, Burger King sells PooPoo Smoothies.

<u>In America we call them Burger King Smoothies.</u>

The snow at the South Pole reflects sound so well you can hear people talking over a mile away.

<u>Too bad there is no one to talk to.</u>

AKB48, japans largest pop group has 89 members.

<u>Look, if you need 89 people to hit the notes you need......to give up.</u>

According to the Mayan calendar, the next time the "world is going to end" is May 3 7138.

<u>Good thing I plan on dying the year prior.</u>

On June 28, 2009, Stephen Hawking hosted a party for time travelers from the future and no one showed up.

<u>And that is because no time traveler would be caught dead at an Applebee's.</u>

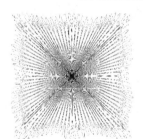

Falling in love costs you on average, two close friends.

<u>So, you shouldn't worry about falling in love.</u>

In ancient Rome, fathers had the legal right to kill their own children.

It's still legal......if you don't get caught.

In the winter of 1918, half of the children in Berlin were suffering from rickets.

And the other half had it they just didn't bitch about it.

The ancient Romans ate puppies.

I bet it tasted like Shit-Zu.

No one knows why we yawn.

But I know you just did it.

Hamsters blink one eye at a time.

Yea...that's called winking.

Americans over 75 watch twice as much TV as teenagers.

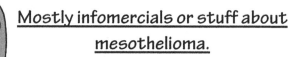

Mostly infomercials or stuff about mesothelioma.

A quarter of all the vegetables eaten in the USA is French fries.

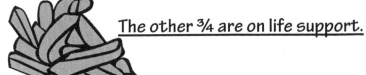

The other ¾ are on life support.

Jaguars are attracted by Calvin Klein's Obsession for Men.

Which means all jaguars are gay?

1 in 9 Honduran men will be murdered.

And 9 in 1 Honduran men is a train.

When the Arctic Monkeys formed, none of them could play an instrument.

Some would say they still can't.

A cow with a name produces 450 more pints of milk a year than one without a name.

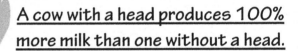

<u>A cow with a head produces 100% more milk than one without a head.</u>

Pregnant women are 42% more likely to be in a car crash but less likely to die, than men of the same age.

<u>I'm shocked we haven't heard a lot about the car crashed pregnant men.</u>

Traffic lights were introduced 18 years before the car was invented.

<u>Just to let the horses know they were about to be obsolete.</u>

A group of pigeons regularly boards the London Underground at Hammersmith and fly off at Ladbroke Grove.

<u>And they don't pay, what kind of liberal shit is this?</u>

To perfect Hercule Poirot's walk, actor David Suchet clasped a coin between his butt.

So, when a review read "he walks like he's got a stick up his ass", they were close.

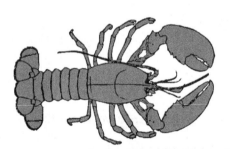 

Lobsters listen with their legs.

Which is why they are so nervous, they always hear footsteps.

The human brain cannot feel pain.

<u>Bullshit…. drink a Slurpee fast.</u>

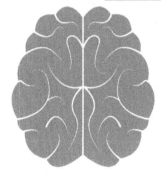

50,000 Korans are buried, each with a white shroud, in the mountains of Pakistan.

<u>Because they realized a book is a shitty gift.</u>

Whoopi Goldberg used to be a bricklayer.

<u>She also used to be funny.</u>

Thanks to their happy meals McDonalds is the largest distributor of toys in the world.

 <u>Take that Santa Claus!!</u>

In 2000 the world's largest iceberg set off from Antarctica.

But we don't know where it's going because it didn't give anyone an itinerary.

Japan has twice as many holidays as the United Kingdom.

That is why they have so much time to blur out their porn.

If you spray pink fabric dye on mulberry plants and feed it to silk worms, they will produce pink silk.

And if you use that silk to make a shirt, then thank you for supporting breast cancer awareness.

Gray whales always mate in a threesome with two males and one female.

As do women without father figures.

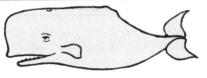

"Response to Those Who Criticize Me for Spending Money on Old Wine & Prostitutes" is a lost work from one of Socrates' disciples.

<u>Wouldn't have been lost had it been called "Old Wine & Prostitutes."</u>

In 2014 the mayor of Brussels donated his underwear to the Brussels Underpants museum, and then they were stolen.

<u>I believe he took them back so that he could cover his Mayor of Brussels Sprouts.</u>

Due to a shortage of official swordsman, Saudi Arabia is considering stopping execution by beheading.

<u>Shocking it's not by the fact that it is fucking barbaric.</u>

56% of British airline pilots have admitted to falling asleep and 29% say that they've woken up to find their co-pilot sleeping.

<u>This would explain why they needed help in WW2.</u>

Men whose initials have positive connotations, like LOV or WIN, live 4.5 years longer than those with negative ones, like BAD or PIG.

And men with initials like SLT or CNT want nothing to do with U.

Bananas are considered unlucky on fishing boats.

Because what if a fish slips on a peel and breaks its neck?

New Zealand's 90-Mile Beach is actually 55 miles long.

<u>Unless you backtrack 35 miles.</u>

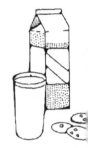

The U.S. Doubled in size after Reagan expanded its coastal waters by 197 nautical miles.

<u>And my cousin doubled in size when Oreo doubled its line of flavors.</u>

Men outnumber women 17 to 1 in Vatican City.

<u>Imagine that ratio if you could be gay.</u>

The first sketch of the Mini-Cooper was drawn on a napkin in Switzerland.

<u>They should have seen the irony and done it on a Maxi-pad.</u>

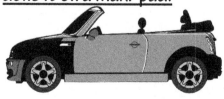

In German things "go like warm rolls" and not "sell like hot cakes"

<u>So…they can use those ovens for something good then?</u>

Coyotes in the United States have learned how traffic lights work so that they can cross the street safely.

<u>But they still start to cross when the clock has 3 seconds left</u>

The average pigeon has 1.6 feet.

After that kitchen accident my uncle is now a pigeon!

A lobster's brain is in its throat.

Which is why they only think of food.

Lee Harvey Oswald still owes an overdue book to the Dallas Public Library.

<u>I don't think he can give it back.</u>

Phil Collins divorced his second wife by fax machine.

<u>She heard it coming in the air that night.</u>

13% of Greek children have dimpled cheeks.

<u>And the other 87% make fun of them.</u>

The notebooks of United States astronauts were fireproofed by seaweed from the Isle of Lewis.

<u>This is only because there is none on the Isle of Clark.</u>

Flor de Guia cheese from the Canary Islands must only be made by women.

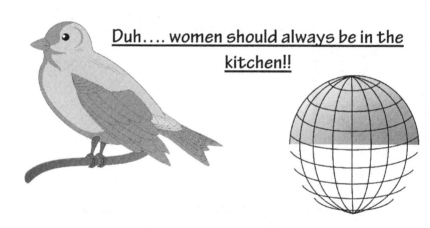

Duh.... women should always be in the kitchen!!

The closer to the equator a woman is, the more likely she is to give birth to a girl.

The further away she is, the closer she is to the pole.

Britons are the most lactose-intolerant people on the planet.

And they are also the most British.

The world has 2 earthquakes every single minute.

Which means your mom takes 2 steps every 60 seconds.

Wherever it is in the world a leaf's internal temperature is always 70 degrees.

<u>Unless you throw it in a volcano.</u>

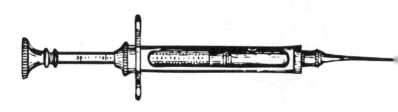

The drugs used for lethal injection cost $83.

<u>A bullet is what? 84 cents?</u>

The "Just Missed It Club" was for people who almost sailed on the Titanic.

<u>And the "Should Have Missed It Club"
is full of frozen corpses.</u>

Guinness isn't black; it is very dark red.

<u>Which, if you think about it, means it
still tastes like shit.</u>

Three Russian cosmonauts who died before re-entry in 1971 are the only human beings to have died outside the earth's atmosphere.

Only if you don't count the documentary Star Wars.

Male squirrels can perform fellatio on themselves.

And all male humans have tried to.

A stressed or sick octopus will sometimes bite off its own limbs.

Just give them some Xanax.

The Greek philosopher Heraclitus attempted to cure an illness by lying in the sun covered in cow dung and died the next day.

Sometimes I don't even need to write a punchline.

In 1944, 9 US airmen were shot down over Chichi Jima the only survivor was George H.W. Bush.

<u>Goes to show what you can do with 2 middle names.</u>

When Canada's northwest territories were divided in two, people voted to keep the old name, the runner up was "Bob".

<u>So basically, Canada got it wrong.</u>

"Last shake o' the bag" was a Victorian
saying for "youngest Child"

Now we just say, "little princess who
can do no wrong even though they
never listen" and no… I have no
resentment towards my sister.

At any one point there are over 100k ships
at sea.

And the Titanic accounts for .7 and .3
of one of them.

There are over 1,000 species of banana and we only eat one of them.

<u>I'm to mad that the government kept 999 bananas a secret to even be funny.</u>

Queen Victoria once had a novelty bustle that played "God Save the Queen" when she sat down.

<u>I would have chosen Queen's "Fat Bottom Girls"</u>

In 2011 scientists re-measured Norway's beaches, islands, and fjords adding over 11,000 miles to its coastline.

<u>Crazy right? Who knew fjord was a word?</u>

People who pirate music also buy more legal music than those who don't.

<u>I only pirate music because I am the captain now.</u>

The current Earl of Sandwich runs a chain of sandwich shops that are called "The Earl of Sandwich".

<u>And president Trump runs a chain of hotels called "Bankruptcy".</u>

In 2006 the most popular name for a cow in Switzerland was Fiona.

<u>No wonder my ex was named Fiona.</u>

The USA and 3 others are the only countries without mandatory maternity leave.

<u>Which sounds right. What gives preggos the right to not work? Way to go USA!!!</u>

By the time children are eight they have forgotten 60% of what happened before they were three.

<u>And by the time you're 90 you forget 100% of what you're doing naked at the park.</u>

In 1989 a Russian psychic was killed by a train while trying to prove he could stop one with his mind.

<u>This one is already funny.</u>

Apple Inc. didn't invent the mouse, but they bought the rights for $40,000.

<u>And Microsoft bought the lefts for $30,000.</u>

Deliveries by pigeon post during World War 2 were 95% successful.

The other 5% were described as delicious.

In 1910 the average Briton sent 116 items by mail.

And in 1911 they all arrived.

Philip Larkin and Kingsley Amis signed off letters to each other with the word "bum".

Similarly, my mom finishes of conversations with my dad with "asshole".

90% of office thermostats in the US. Don't work.

Neither do 90% of the employees.

Charlotte Bronte was the first person to use the terms "raised eyebrow" and "Wild West".

Which goes to show that if you work hard, you too can be forgotten.

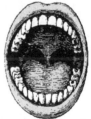

In 1920, Clarence Blethen retired hurt from a baseball game after he bit himself on the bottom with false teeth he kept in his back pocket.

Brings a new meaning to the phrase "Bite Me".

90% of the men in Paraguay died in the war of the Triple Alliance.

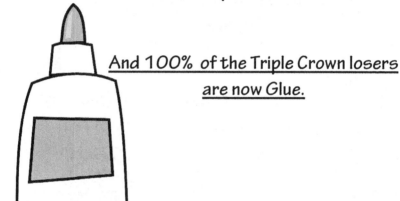

And 100% of the Triple Crown losers are now Glue.

After the Battle of Hastings, King Harold's body was identified by the tattoo of his wife's name above his heart.

She was named "I signed a prenup, she gets nothing".

Chinese eunuchs kept their testicles in a jar in hopes they will reattach them in the next world.

<u>I thought it was to give them to their wives, so they would fit better in their purses.</u>

Prisoners on Alcatraz always had hot showers, so they didn't get acclimated to cold water and try to escape by swimming.

<u>What I'm hearing is CRIMINALS go hot water, but I can't get any in my apartment!!</u>

Henry VIII's lavatory at Hampton court was known as "The Great House of Easement."

His plumber called it "The Great House of Excrement"

The phrase "pipe dream" comes from the fantasies induced by smoking opium.

And now it's used to describe my grandma's glaucoma medication.

Edouard Manet's cat was eaten during the Siege of Paris in 1870.

Since it was France it was served with a nice sauce.

During the Vietnam War, each US soldier took around 40 amphetamine tablets a year.

Including the ones in the reserves back home.

The first Mc Donald's only sold hot dogs.

This stopped because the name
McWeiner didn't sell.

In 2002 the US military developed a
sandwich that will stay fresh for three
years.

And in 2005 they found out they
actually didn't.

Human rights were invented in Iran in the sixth century.

<u>Too bad they don't consider women to be humans.</u>

Forest fires can be sparked by sunlight magnified by water on dried out leaves.

<u>So.... water is trying to kill us......</u>

When the Hindenburg exploded, 62 of the 97 passengers survived.

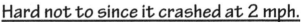

Hard not to since it crashed at 2 mph.

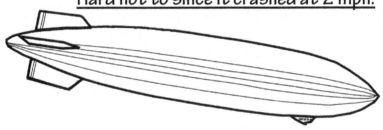

The word for "carp" in Montenegro is "Krap"

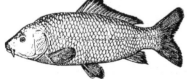

Which makes sense cause carp are shitty fish.

Icebergs make a crackling sound known as "blergy seltzer"

Most people refer to it as "FUCK its breaking!! Get off this damn thing!!!"

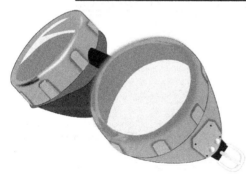

The first snow goggles were made of polished caribou antler.

I bet they were actually made from a guy looking through his hands when he wasn't prepared.

The largest lizard in Australia is as fast as Usain Bolt.

<u>But if you put his gold medal on it, it would get squished.</u>

In 18th century America, Thanksgiving was celebrated with a day of fasting and a prayer.

<u>Now we just gorge and pray we don't explode.</u>

Species of bat include the wrinkle-faced bat, thumb-less bat, and flower-faced bat.

I feel like these bats got super bullied in school.

The hairs on a raspberry are female.

And they from a landing strip.

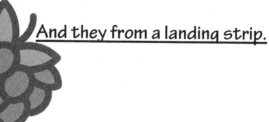

Avocados are toxic to horses.

<u>But its quicker to use a rifle.</u>

Eating dogs is legal in 44 US states.

<u>But it makes me wonder why it isn't in the other 10.</u>

You can tell if someone is yawning from their eyes alone.

But only if they are still in the person.

Hamsters can store over half their weight in food in their cheeks.

Sounds impressive until you realize they weigh 6 oz.

1/3 of British office workers have the same thing for lunch every day.

<u>And since its British, yes, it's disgusting.</u>

A vegetable is 4 times healthier than a fruit.

<u>But fruits are so much more mobile than vegetables.</u>

The Aztec culture wore necklaces made of popcorn.

<u>Which means classrooms around Christmas are considered culturally appropriated.</u>

A "singlewoman" is a medieval slang for a prostitute.

<u>Now its slang for one- woman.</u>

An Atlantic salmon's sense of smell is over 1,000 times stronger than a dog.

<u>Only cause if a dog smells in water it drowns.</u>

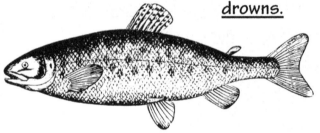

Every day the human body makes 300 billion new cells.

<u>So, if you ever think that you are not that special, remember, you're not.</u>

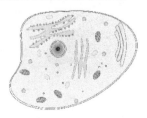

Croquet was dropped as an Olympic sport after 1900 cause only 1 spectator came to watch.

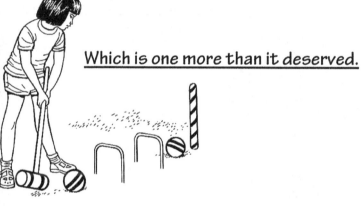

<u>Which is one more than it deserved.</u>

The tobacco hornworm uses its disgusting breath to fend of predators.

<u>So, does my sister.</u>

Only 1% of a tree is alive.

<u>So is my grandma......she's on life support.</u>

Charitable donations of clothing to Africa have led to the collapse of its textile industry.

<u>See America? HELPING HURTS!!</u>

Scotland has the biggest bog in Europe.

<u>This just in…. Who cares?</u>

"Empty" was originally spelled emty.

<u>Let's go back!! Its shorter it'll save time!!</u>

There is a 12% chance that a game of Monopoly will *go* on forever.

<u>So that's an 88% chance of someone getting pissed and throwing the game board.</u>

Guinness isn't suitable for vegans because it contains traces of fish bladder.

<u>Vegans aren't the only ones grossed out by that.</u>

If all the salt in the oceans were spread evenly over the land it would be 500 feet tall.

But you can take that with a grain of salt.

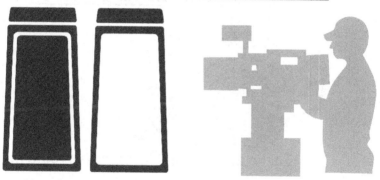

When he was president of Venezuela Hugo Chavez hosted a show show Called Alo Presednte.

Trump should start one called Lunatics at 11.

Human Brains are 10% smaller than they were 21,000 years ago.

<u>And that started to change with the introduction of the Kardashians.</u>

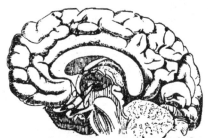

There are 100,000 more bicycles in Amsterdam than there are people.

<u>Which is what happens when you get high and have access to the internet.</u>

Barry Manilow's No. 1 hit "I Write the Songs" wasn't written by him.

New buildings in New York City must have twice as many women's toilets as men's.

We need to stop this and have men's toilet equality!!

Switzerland monitors its airspace around the clock but only intercepts illegal flights during its office hours.

<u>So just learn the office hours and transport your drugs around them!</u>

When neuroscientist James Fallon studied the brain scans of murders compared to his, he discovered he was a psychopath.

<u>His wife and children will be sadly missed.</u>

Hummingbirds lay eggs the size of peas.

<u>Which is why it takes 3,000 to make an Omelet.</u>

If you stood on the Martian equator at noon, it would feel like summer at your feet and winter at your head.

<u>And if you did a hand stand you could sing "Flaming head, shoulders knees are froze".</u>

William Buckland was expelled from the shrine of St. Rosalia for pointing out that her bones were of a goat.

<u>The skull with horns shoulda given that away 1st no?</u>

In Inuit languages, the closest word to "freedom" is annakpok, which translates to "not caught".

<u>In Russian the closest word to freedom is Svoboda, which means "election Tampering".</u>

In the French Revolution, prisoners were taken to the guillotine on wagons used to transport cow dung.

<u>That's a shitty way to go out.</u>

The bell rung to mark the death of Ivan the Terrible's son was tried for treason and exiled to Siberia.

<u>Taco bell should be charged with 10 million cases of IBS.</u>

Karl Lagerfeld's cat has 2 maids that write down everything it does in a book.

<u>He was shocked to find out it pawned all his valuables.</u>

Vegetarian sausages were first patented in Britain in 1918 by Konrad Adenauer.

<u>And since 1918....no one has liked them.</u>

The Hindenburg airship was almost called the Hitler.

If so they could have gotten rid of the hydrogen and just had him blowing his hot air to give it lift.

Barf is "snow in Persian.

Threw me off when they tried to sell me a Barfcone.

Britain's biggest pig contains enough pork to make 6,000 sausages.

<u>You could probably get 7,000 out of my uncle.</u>

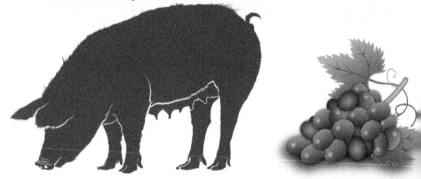

Grapples are grape flavored apples.

<u>And sadly, you can't use them to scale a castle.</u>

Phillip is Greek for "horse lover".

I knew that guy Phil was off....

Valentine's Day is banned in Iran and Saudi Arabia.

Cause if cupid flies in the middle east he will get hit by a drone.

In Peter Pan, Peter "thinned out" the lost boys when they got too old.

<u>He did this by putting them in lower paying jobs in his peanut butter factories.</u>

The builders of the Great Wall of China were fed on sauerkraut.

<u>Which is why they got it done so quickly, to stop eating that nasty shit.</u>

Over 2.8 million American dogs are on anti-depressants.

<u>As are their pretentious white owners.</u>

By the time they leave high school American children will have eaten around 1,500 peanut butter and jelly sandwiches.

<u>And if they are allergic to peanut butter.... its natural selection.</u>

Astronaut Harrison Schmitt was allergic to the moon.

<u>We know because he took off his helmet to smell the moon and died.</u>

America drinks more wine than France

<u>Only because we've mastered the best box of it.</u>

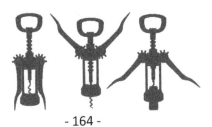

Corn, avocados, and peas are fruits, not vegetables.

My gay cousin got hit by a car and is now both.

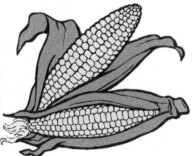

Un-popped popcorn kernels are called "spinsters."

I call them "Dammit, you cracked my damn tooth!!"

88% of women routinely wear shoes that are too small for their feet.

<u>Which could explain why they're always pissy.</u>

New research shows that, for luxury brands, ruder staff equals higher sales.

<u>My ex would make a killing.</u>

Termites like the smell of newspaper ink.

<u>And my uncle loves the smell of Sharpies.</u>

Nasa estimates that near-earth asteroid Eros contains around 20 billion tons of gold.

<u>Donald trump wants us to get it so he can make more of his hair.</u>

The first man to swim the whole length of Britain grew a beard to protect his face from jellyfish.

<u>Too bad they still stung his forehead.</u>

3,079 chemicals have been identified in human urine.

<u>And if you put them together they taste like piss.</u>

Virtually all Koreans lack the gene that produces bad smelling armpits.

<u>Thus, the reason for unscented deodorant.</u>

Mosquito sperm have a sense of smell.

<u>Its favorite smell is raw eggs.</u>

Boys in Bronze Age Russia had to slay their own dogs to prove they were warriors.

<u>Isn't that what Jeffery Dahmer did?</u>

There are more Internet hosts in Manhattan than all of Africa.

<u>Only cause it's hard to equip a satellite dish to a cheetah.</u>

There are more stretch limos in Glasgow than Los Angeles.

Only cause their obese population stretched them out.

In 2008 Scotland spent $ 186,000 coming up with a new slogan, it was "welcome to Scotland."

And if you've been there you know it should have been called "Why are you here? Italy is so much cooler."

"Misspell" is one of the most commonly misspelled words in English.

<u>Not for me though, I never mispell it.</u>

The word "twelve" is worth 12 points in a game of Scrabble.

<u>And if you knew that, then what is it like not having friends??</u>

The largest known prime number is over 16 million digits long.

<u>I thought the largest known Prime was Optimus.</u>

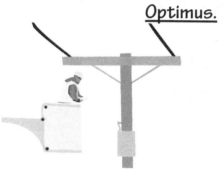

Offa's Dyke was built 200 years before King Offa was born.

<u>So, then they named the King after a dyke….?</u>

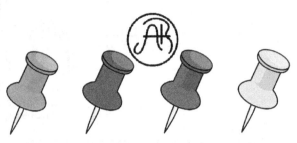

In Sweden, an Indian burn is known as a "thousand-needle prank."

Know why? Cause they aren't racist like the U.S.

In 2007 police in Iran detained 14 squirrels suspected of spying.

They were guilty and had a moose as an accomplice.

In the Norwegian town of Longyearbyen, it is against the law to die.

<u>And the punishment is death.</u>

In 2013 a Judge in Michigan found himself in contempt of court when his own phone went off during a trial.

<u>But he gave himself a light sentence.</u>

When being photographed Victorians said "prunes" to look more serious.

Now the Victorians say nothing when being photographed since they're dead.

The coastline of Norway is long enough to circle the planet over 2 times.

But only once around your mom.

In 1922, Ernest Hemingway's wife lost his entire life's work by leaving it on a train.

And shockingly they still haven't found her body.

American tank crews have a superstition that will not allow them to eat or even say the word apricot on board the tank.

Only because tanks are allergic to them.

In 2014 scientists found over 700 new planets in a single day.

But none of them have brought more joy than Uranus.

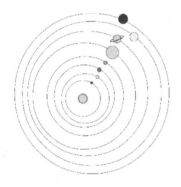

Scatomancy is telling the future by looking at turds.

What the actual fuck?

In the General Election of 1741 candidates in London were pelted with dead dogs and cats.

Which is where we got that saying…." If you get hit with dead animals, you smell like shit."

In 2013, Hanukkah and Thanksgiving began on the same day.

And they sang "Dreidel Dreidel Dreidel I made you out of…." And then passed out because of the L-Tryptophan in the turkey.

If you exposed a diamond on a tanning bed, it would eventually evaporate, but it would take 10 million years.

If you put a person on a tanning bed it will eventually become a star on Jersey Shore.

Human teeth evolved from fish scales.

And we have primate DNA.... Does that make us Sea Monkeys?

Without bats there would be no tequila,
because they pollinate the agave plants.

Which is why Bruce Wayne loves margaritas.

More than 5,000 Swedish men have the
first name Love.

I hoooope one of their last names is Stick.

Babies can hear dog whistles.

What baby did they ask to find this out?

Alan Shepard took a peanut to the Moon.

But one of the other astronauts was allergic so now they only get pretzels.

George H.W. Bush wears socks with his own
face on them.

<u>They are of Skeletons</u>

My Acknowledgements!!!

I acknowledge that Shin Ramen on La Brea between Sunset and Hollywood Blvd. is the best ramen house in LA.

I acknowledge all my friends and people that say they liked my show after a show. Those little compliments mean the world.

I acknowledge anyone who follows me on social media (everything is @1AndrewRose) and likes what I do.

I acknowledge that I one day want to be on a first name basis with The Rock.

I also acknowledge that I have grown as a comedian and have gotten commendations from my friends and peers which means the world.

More importantly I acknowledge that I have grown as a person. Mainly because I have been going to the gym more, so my muscles are fairly bigger.

I love you all, be on the lookout for Vol. 3 Coming out in 2020!!!

About the Author

Andrew Rose is a standup comedian originally from Oklahoma currently residing in Los Angeles California.

(This is the same stuff as was in the last book if you care)

He was the host of The World Series of Comedy, tours the country telling jokes, and can be seen on his Instagram page posting his Random Facts of The Day, which is the basis for this book.

If you got this far into the book give him a text at

1-914-432-2662 and let him know what you thought of it.

(Yes, it is my actual number, and sadly only one person messaged me last time and they didn't respond to my query so be more vigilant than them, and say something)

This is Andrew

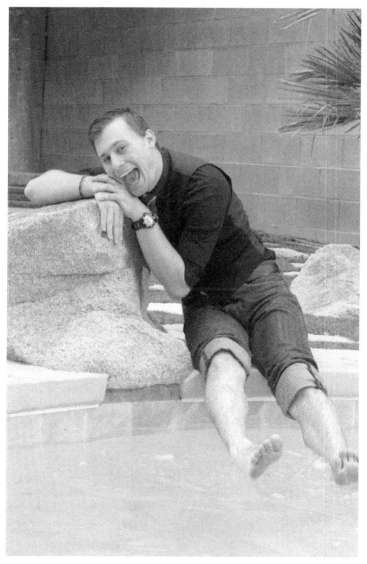

Did you get the last volume of this book series and write in this section of the book?

Well? Are you going to answer
that page over there??

Made in the USA
Coppell, TX
12 December 2020